Barn Cats of Colorado

skunk and chauncey

by Jordan Wunderlich

right, 2018, Jordan Wunderlich

The story of Skunk and Chauncey...

Skunk and Chauncey were found hiding behind a hay bale as kittens. Their little mews and tiny heads poking around the corner of the bale made it a bit of a poor hiding place... But they were scared and hungry and didn't know what to do...

I quickly found out why that was.

I found their mother's body a half mile away.

And from that sadness came a new life.

Skunk and Chauncey were adopted by the lady whose hay they were hiding behind and became barn cats!

They now spend their days wandering around the barn and land, hunting the little rodents who scurry around, and... harassing me at every opportunity.

Outtakes

www.ingramcontent.com/pod-product-compliance
Lightning Source LLC
Chambersburg PA
CBHW041154290426
44108CB00002B/62